The Little Junk Music

Making music with found objects - activities for the Foundation Stage

Written by Simon MacDonald
Illustrations by Martha Hardy

The Little Book of Junk Music
ISBN 1 904187 87 0

©Featherstone Education Ltd, 2004
Text © Simon MacDonald, 2004
Series editor, Sally Featherstone

First published in the UK, February 2004
'Little Books' is a trade mark of Featherstone Education Ltd.

Published in the United Kingdom by
Featherstone Education Ltd.
44 - 46 High Street
Husbands Bosworth
Leicestershire
LE17 6LP

Contents

Introduction

The activities in this book are intended to help you to plan musical experiences which are easy to resource and enjoyable for both you and the children.

The most common format for these activities is a circle, and there is guidance on ways to organise children into circles for activities. Sometimes, activities will follow a more processional path around the space or setting; and other activities offer children freer exploration of the space as individuals or in small groups.

Work in this area is equally appealing to children as young as three and as old as eighteen. Obviously, the younger the group the more supervision and support they need. For example, in a nursery setting the activities work very well when the children are in their key worker groups. Practitioners in Reception classes are advised to use additional adults wherever possible to increase support or to enable groupings to be smaller. In this way, all children will have opportunities to be involved and to discuss the sounds and music they make.

The Little Book of Junk Music is divided into the following sections:

Part 1 focuses on circle chants and rhymes:
  sound exploration using voice and body parts
  sounds from letters/animals/vehicles
  call and response chants

Part 2 emphasises body rhythms:
  clapping, tapping, stamping, clicking etc
  passing rhythms using hand claps/rubs/finger clicks, stamps, etc.
  using body sounds to accompany and create songs and stories

Part 3 encourages the exploration of textures and surfaces:
  sound exploration using different textures and surfaces
  experimenting using beating, rubbing, tapping, dropping etc.

Part 4 explores the use of simple beaters and found objects both inside and outside your setting.

Part 5 extends Junk Music into the use of more familiar everyday objects, and putting these together to make a Junk Orchestra. Use newspaper, fabric scraps, buckets, stiff brushes, old clothes, brooms, balls, plastic bottles filled with water or other materials such as sand, marbles, earth, ball bearings to add to your range of sound makers.

Part 6 covers putting all the sounds together to create sound environments to accompany longer stories, dance sessions and other situations.

We have also included some guidance on using impromptu music to celebrate the learning, the events and the festivals within your setting, by having parades and processions!

Finally, there is guidance on how children can make their own simple instruments from found materials.

5

Links with the Foundation Stage

Music is a truly cross curricular activity, enhancing every area of learning. Singing, listening, maintaining a rhythm, enhancing feelings, moving and dancing are all ways in which practitioner exploit the benefits of music. Here are some of the key links with the Foundation Curriculum and the Early Learning Goals. Of course, there are more!
A few of the statements from the Stepping Stones accompany each activity to help you with planning and assessment for the Profile.

PERSONAL, SOCIAL & EMOTIONAL DEVELOPMENT
   * continue to be interested, excited & motivated to learn
   * be confident to try new activities
   * maintain attention, concentration & sit quietly when appropriate
   * respond to significant experiences, showing a range of feelings
   * have a developing respect for their own cultures & beliefs &
      those of other people
   * form good relationships with adults & peers
   * work as part of a group or class, taking turns & sharing fairly
   * select & use activities & resources independently
COMMUNICATION, LANGUAGE AND LITERACY
   * sustain attentive listening, responding to what they have heard
      by relevant comments, questions or actions
   * listen with enjoyment and respond to stories, songs, and other
      music, rhymes and poems and make up their own stories,
      rhymes and poems
   * explore and experiment with sounds, words and texts stories,
KNOWLEDGE & UNDERSTANDING OF THE WORLD
   * investigate objects & materials by using all of their senses as
      appropriate
   * find out about, & identify some features of objects and events
      they observe
   * ask questions about why things happen & how things work

PHYSICAL DEVELOPMENT
* move with confidence, imagination & in safety
* move with control and co-ordination
* use a range of small and large equipment
* handle tools, objects etc. safely and with increasing control

CREATIVE DEVELOPMENT
* recognise and explore how sounds can be changed, sing simple songs from memory, recognise repeated sounds & sound patterns & match movements to music
* use their imagination in music, dance, imaginative & role play & stories
* respond in a variety of ways to what they see, hear, smell, touch and feel;
* express & communicate their ideas, thoughts and feelings by using a widening range of materials, suitable tools, imaginative and role play, movement, designing and making, and a variety of songs and instruments.

Making circles for music activities

Children need to learn how to make a circle quickly and quietly. An effective way to help them is to sing the following song as each child finds a person to hold hands with. The circle comes together as they sing:

'Come and make a circle,
Come and make a circle,
Come and make a circle just like we've done before.

Do it very quietly,
Do it very quietly,
Do it very quietly just like we've done before.

Sit down very quietly,
Sit down very quietly,
Sit down very quietly just like we've done before.'

Part 1

Chant it! – Exploring sounds and chants

– using voices to explore rhythm, gesture and movement

Using Nursery Rhymes

Links with ELGs
CLL - Enjoy rhythmic activities,
PD - Respond to rhythm by means of gesture and movement.
CD - Respond to sound, show an interest in what they hear

What you need
No special equipment

1. Ask the children to choose a song or nursery rhyme.
2. Sing the song once or twice to make sure they know the words.
3. Now explain that you are going to stop in the middle of the song and they must try to remember the word you stopped on.
4. Sing the song again and stop on a word. Make sure the children know which word you have chosen. (eg 'York' in Grand Old Duke of York)
5. Now use this word to make up a chant. Repeat the word over and over again to make the chant. Sometimes say the word fast, sometimes slow. Encourage the children to follow your lead.
6. Now play 'Echo chanting'. You chant the word, then the children copy you like an echo.

Play this game at group time or when you have a few spare minutes.

Using Alphabet Songs

1. Begin by singing your favourite alphabet song, or just chanting the alphabet. Practice it to make sure they know the order.
2. Choose a child to put their hand up when they want to stop at a letter, for example 'O'.
3. Now tell the children that you are going to play with the letter and make it sound different each time they say it.
4. Say the letter fast, slow, high, low or any combination of these - fast and high, slow and low, etc.
5. If the children can cope with more, experiment by starting high and get progressively lower as you repeat it and vice versa.
6. Encourage the group to 'feel' the different sounds by placing their hands on points of resonance on their bodies (heads, faces, chests, etc.)
7. Talk about the feeling of the sound before trying another letter.

Another idea

Play the same game with 3 letter words with a vowel in the middle, such as hat, bat, can, cat, sit etc.

Links with ELGs

CLL - Name letters of alphabet
PD - Respond to rhythm by means of gesture and movement.
CD - Respond to sound, show an interest in what they hear.

What you need
No special equipment

11

Play Names

Start with a circle as before, singing the circle song.

1. Now go round the circle and ask each child in turn to say their name. Practice this till the children can do it quickly.
2. Now ask them to go round again saying their name in the way you suggest (shouting, whispering, giggling, singsong etc). Go round the circle with the same way of saying names for everyone, before making it more difficult.
3. Now make it more difficult in some of these ways:
   * letting the children choose which way they say their name, and copying this.
   * saying their name in a different way from the child before.
   * copying the last child's way of saying their name
   * saying the name of the child next to them

! Remember that younger children will need much more practice and much simpler rules!

Another idea

Play the same game with the names of adults, occupations, pets, birthdays, TV characters etc.

Always ask children's permission before using their name in a chant.

Links with ELGs

PSD - Maintain attention and concentration; take turns
CLL - Sustain attentive listening
PD - Respond to rhythm by gesture & movement.
CD - Respond to sound, show interest in what they hear.

What you need
No special equipment

Tweet, Bark, Moo, and Roar!

Links with ELGs
PSED - Relate to and make attachments with members of a group.
CLL - Join with refrains.
PD - Move body position as necessary
CD - Respond with body movement

What you need
No special equipment

Begin with a circle as before.

1. Take turns to think of an animal sound. Then go round the group, each person making their own sound (don't worry if they copy each other at first!).
2. Now choose one child to send their sound round the circle by repeating it to their neighbour, who repeats it to theirs till it has been round the ring. Repeat with other starter sounds.
3. Make the game more complicated by asking each child to make their own sound, not copy the one before.

Another idea
Play the same game with vehicle sounds, musical instruments etc.

This is another game you can play at group time or when you have a few spare minutes.

Vowel Yowl (suitable for more mature children)

Links with ELGs
CLL - Join songs, rhymes, poems
PD - Respond to rhythm by
gesture and movement.
CD - Respond to sound, show
interest in what they hear.
Recognise repeated sounds
and sound patterns.

What you need
No special equipment

Start with a circle, singing the circle song to help children
to be ready quickly and quietly.

1. Explain the game you are going to play. Give it a name, and
   explain that the game only uses vowels (you may want to have
   a visual clue sheet of the vowels).
2. Ask one child to choose a vowel for the first chant.
3. Play together with this vowel, repeating it in different ways -
   fast 'o.o.o.o.', slow 'oooooo', fast and slow 'o.o.o. ooo.'
4. Continue to play the game with different vowels and different
   speeds. Play 'call and response', with you calling the pattern
   first for the children to follow.
5. Try using two vowel sounds to make patters - eg o.o.o.e.e.e.a.a
6. Now try using your hands to orchestrate the length of the
   letter, move your hands close together for short and further
   apart to make the sound longer. This way you can stretch and
   shorten the sound at will!

Another idea

Play the same game with 3 letter words with a vowel in the
middle, such as hat, bat, can, cat, sit etc.

Part 2

Body rhythms

- using voices and body parts together
for rhythm and movement

Feel it!

Begin with a circle as before.

1. Make sure children know how to play this game safely, not hurting themselves or others by over enthusiastic actions.
2. Repeat Vowel Howl as before, but this time, encourage the children to change the sounds they are making by tapping their cheeks, chests or backs. This will give a 'warbling' sound.
3. Help the children to understand how they can make this 'warbling' louder or softer by the way they tap their bodies.
4. Try 'Meet and greet'. Two children meet in the centre of the ring and greet each other with their own choice of combined sound and warbling.
5. As their confidence grows, they will be able to hold short 'conversations with each other. You could give them key words such as 'happy', 'sad', 'angry' to help them adjust the sounds they make. You will be amazed at the language that emerges as children become more confident.

Another game you can play in spare minutes.

Links with ELGs
CLL - Join repeated refrains.
KUW- Show curiosity & interest by facial expression.
PD - Move body position.
CD - Learn how sounds can be changed.

What you need
No special equipment

16

Lip Smacking Fingers

Links with ELGs

CLL - Distinguish one sound from another.

CD - Respond to sound, show an interest in what they hear.
Explore how sounds can be made and changed.

What you need
No special equipment

Start with a circle, singing the circle song to help children to be ready quickly and quietly.

1. Show the children how they can make a new sound by holding their index finger like a toothbrush in front of their lips and moving it up and down as they say their name. (Older readers may remember this as the sound of the daleks in Doctor Who!)

2. Explore the way this sound can be changed with different words and voice tones. Try swooping from high to low, low to high, long and short sounds.

3. Once the children are used to making this sound, they can try conversations with each other or with you. You could even try doing the register in Lip smacking speech.

Another idea

Try passing a word or phrase around the circle from child to child like in Chinese Whispers. See how the message changes from beginning to end of the circuit.

The Finger Popping Orchestra

What you need
No special equipment

Start with a circle, singing the circle song to help children
to be ready for the activity.

1. The orchestra depends on the sound you make when you put
your index finger in one cheek and pull it out between your
lips with a POP. This action needs practice! Show the children
what to do (or get one of them to demonstrate).
2. Sing 'Pop Goes the Weasel' as a warm up, making the POP at
the appropriate point.
3. When the children can POP on cue, use your finger or a
pointer to point to individuals or groups to POP as you point.
4. When the children can do this (it will take younger children
longer!) you can tap your foot or play some music or nursery
rhymes with a strong beat for your Finger Popping Orchestra
to accompany.

Another idea
Older children can take turns to conduct the orchestra or
some could sing while the others make the POPs.

Clever Clapping, Super Stamping

Begin with a circle as before.

1. The emphasis of this activity is the rhythm that you pass around the group.
2. Tell the children that what you pass them is very valuable and you don't want to lose it.
3. Now pass a simple rhythm round the group, starting with one clap. When this returns to you, add another clap. Young children will be able to manage three claps in a sequence, not usually more, unless they have had plenty of practice with you.
4. When the children can manage three simple claps, try changing the rhythm (eg quick, quick, slow <u>or</u> slow, slow, slow <u>or</u> quick, quick, quick).
5. When the children can carry three claps in different rhythms, stand up and add a stamp or two to the rhythm (eg stamp, clap, clap, <u>or</u> stamp, clap, stamp, or even stamp, clap, stamp, clap).

Encourage the children to be the leader if they want to.
Never force them.

Links with ELGs
PS&ED- Relate & make attachments to members of their group.

CLL - Join in with refrains. Distinguish one sound from another.

PD - Move body position as necessary.

What you need
No special equipment

More Clever Clapping, Super Stamping

This extension activity involves more movement and more noise!

1. Start the activity in a standing circle and ask the children to stay inside the space the circle makes.
2. Show the children these movements:
   * Stamp on alternate feet (called STAMP, STAMP),
   * Slap thighs with both hands twice (SLAP, SLAP),
   * Beat chest twice with fists (THUMP, THUMP),
   * A single clap in front of you (CLAP) - this is the finishing movement of the sequence.
3. Practice this sequence standing in a circle, with you keeping the rhythm and everyone saying the words.
4. When they can follow the rhythm, let them stamp off into the space, keeping the rhythm and the movements correct. They must stop at the end of each sequence.

If they have a problem following, stop and re-establish the beat, or make the sequence shorter.

Another idea

Try doing the sequence several times without stopping. Younger children may find this impossible!

Links with ELGs

PSED- Work in a group.
CLL - Join in with refrains and sequences.
Distinguish one sound or movement from another.
PD - Move body position as necessary.
Use space with care.

What you need

No special equipment

Rainstorm

This activity works best on a hard floor but can still be effective on carpet. Indeed, carpet encourages better listening skills!
* Remind the children not to rub on carpet too fast or it may burn them.

1. Begin by asking the children to kneel in a circle with their hands in their laps. Tell the children that you are going to make a rainstorm together, but it is going to start little by little.
2. The activity works best when each sound is passed round the circle. As each child joins in the volume rises.
3. Show the children how to put their hands together as if they are going to dive into the sea, and then rub them together. This makes the wind, rushing across the sky and the clouds racing overhead.
4. Now tell them that it's starting to rain. Tap your fingers (index and middle) on the floor.
5. The rain is starting to fall harder now. Tap all your fingers on the floor. Add some rubbing too.
6. Now the rain is really hard. It's pouring! Slap your thighs.
7. Oh no! It's raining harder than ever now! Clap your hands fast.
8. Gently bring the storm to a close by reversing the actions - clap hands, slap thighs, tap all fingers, tap two fingers and finally rub hands. Add a commentary by saying that the rainstorm is over.

Hey! My Name's Joe - an action song

This all-action song requires a combination of dexterity and stamina!
It is also a lot of fun and will have the children falling about with laughter.
Parents and carers will love you for teaching their children this song, they
will not be able to resist joining in themselves. Start by singing the circle
song to help children to be <u>sitting</u> quickly and quietly.

Links with ELGs

PS&ED- Relate and make attachments to members of their group.

CLL - Join in with refrains. Distinguish one sound from another.

PD - Move body position.

CD - Enjoy joining in with songs and ring games.

Verse 1

Hey! My name's Joe,
I work in a button factory.
I've got a wife and no kids.
One day the boss said to me,
He said "Joe, Are you busy?"
I said "No",
He said "Put your finger on this button".
(Start thrusting arm forward with index finger pointing)

Verse 2

Hey! My name's Joe,
I work in a button factory.
I've got a wife and ONE kid.
One day the boss said to me,
He said "Joe, Are you busy?"
I said "No"
He said "Put your finger on this button".
(Start thrusting other arm forward as well,
with index finger pointing)

Verse 3

Hey! My name's Joe,
I work in a button factory.
I've got a wife and TWO kids.
One day the boss said to me,
He said "Joe, Are you busy?"
I said "No".
He said "Put your foot on this button".
(Keep thrusting both arms forward, and start moving one leg back and forward, ending with a stamp. You can stand up for this bit if you like!).

Verses 5, 6 and 7

In verse four, Joe has THREE kids and has to put his OTHER FOOT on a button.
In verse five, Joe has FOUR kids and has to put his HEAD on a button.
In verse six, Joe has FIVE kids and has to put his TONGUE on a button.
(By this time, the children will be using both arms, both legs, their head and their tongue).

and finally Joe says

Hey! My name's Joe,
I work in a button factory.
I've got a wife and SIX kids.
One day the boss said to me,
He said "Joe, Are you busy?"
I said "YES".
(By this time, the children will probably need a rest!).

Echo Rhyme - Lock and Key

Links with ELGs
CLL - Join in with repeated refrains.

CD - Respond to sound with body movement.

Enjoy joining in with dancing & ring games.

Repeat words and actions

What you need
No special equipment

Echo Rhyme - Lock and Key

1. Start with a circle, and establish a rhythm by clapping gently before you start the rhyme.

2. Explain that the game is an echo game - they need to listen to you and repeat what you say, only changing 'lock' to 'key'.

    ADULT: I am a brass lock

    CHILDREN: I am a brass key

    ADULT: I am a paper lock

    CHILDREN: I am a paper key

    ADULT: I am a wooden lock

    CHILDREN: I am a wooden key

    ADULT: I am a mon lock

    CHILDREN: I am a mon-key

    You can repeat the rhyme using different materials or it can be changed to trick the children into saying tur-key, don-key or han-ky.

Boom-chicka-rocka-chicka-rocka-chicka-boom

Here is another response rhyme:

ADULT: Boom!
CHILDREN: Boom!
ADULT: Boom-chicka!
CHILDREN: Boom-chicka!
ADULT: Boom-chicka-rocka!
CHILDREN: Boom-chicka-rocka!
ADULT: Boom-chicka-rocka-chicka-rocka!
CHILDREN: Boom-chicka-rocka-chicka-rocka!
ADULT: Boom-chicka-rocka-chicka-rocka-chicka-boom!
CHILDREN: Boom-chicka-rocka-chicka-rocka-chicka-boom!
ADULT: Aha!
CHILDREN: Aha!
ADULT: Oh Yeah!
CHILDREN: Oh Yeah!
ADULT: Once more!
CHILDREN: Once more!

Try saying this rhyme really fast, really slow, really sad, really quiet.

Links with ELGs

CLL - Join repeated refrains.
KUW- Show curiosity & interest by facial expression.
PD - Move body position.
CD - Learn how sounds can be changed.

What you need
No special equipment

25

About Part 3

Before using the activities in the next section, you will need to prepare yourself by looking closely at the materials you might use from your setting. The activities in Section 2 use familiar objects and materials, most of which you will already have. However, it is wise to make sure these items are not already full of something else, or on an inaccessible shelf in a cupboard or needing to be borrowed from older children!

You will also need to explain to the children that you are going to explore the different sounds that can be found around your setting or classroom. You can prepare the children for more complex activities by some of the following simple tasks or challenges:

* finding an object in the room that can be tapped or knocked with a hand or finger to produce a sound.
* going on a sound making walk around the room, the hall, the cloakroom or the garden, to see how many sound makers you can find there.
* using these sound makers to accompany familiar nursery rhymes and songs (eg Miss Polly had a Dolly; 1, 2, 3, 4, 5; Johnny Hammers with One Hammer).
* using the sound makers to make your own compositions with loud and soft sounds, fast and slow passages.
* making a music corner or music basket for outside, containing some of the 'found' sound makers.
* using the sound makers for sound effects in stories (from books or ones you have made up together).

This way, children get used to using sound effects and found musical instruments as a natural part of learning.

Part 3

Exploring sounds

- using textures and surfaces

Rubber Rulers and Super Sticks

Children should be trained to use sticks and rulers safely. Make sure they know the safety rules!

1. Put the sticks in the middle of the circle or on a table.
2. Invite a few children to choose an instrument and hold it still in their hands.
3. Ask the other children to watch carefully.
4. Now let the children with instruments make sounds with them in any (safe) way they can think of - tapping, scraping, rubbing on different surfaces. Let them go outside the circle if they wish.
5. When they stop (at your hand signal), talk about what you heard. Ask some individuals to demonstrate their sounds.
6. Now let another group have a go. This time the audience could close their eyes and see if they can tell who made which sound, and how.

This may be too difficult for the youngest children!

Another idea

If you think the children can manage it, introduce the idea of 'pinging' the ruler by holding it over the edge of the table and using one hand to hold and the other to 'ping'. Make some music, movement or a story by combining 'pinging' and the other noises you have discovered.

Links with ELGs

CLL - Distinguish one sound from another.

CD - Explore and learn how sounds can be changed.

What you need

* Rulers, flat pieces of batten, sticks

Sandy Sounds

Links with ELGs

CLL - Distinguish one sound from another.

CD - Respond and show an interest in what they hear. Explore and learn how sounds can change.

What you need

* Sandpapers in different sizes, shapes, textures
* A strong cloth bag
* A 'pointing wand' or stick

Sandpaper comes in many different grades and shape for different sorts of machines. Try to get some discs and sanding blocks as well.

1. Put a selection of sandpapers in the bag (enough for two pieces each), and make a circle on the carpet or floor.
2. Sing this song to the tune of 'London Bridge is falling Down'.
   Pass around the music bag
   Music bag, music bag,
   Pass around the music bag
   Who will play our game?
3. On the last line, just like Pass the Parcel, whoever has the bag may take a maximum of two pieces of sandpaper from the bag. Repeat the song until all the children have some sandpaper.
4. Now give the children some time to feel the sandpapers and experiment with making sounds.
5. Use your 'pointing wand' to indicate which child can make their sound. You could choose two or three to play together sometimes. Make sure everyone has time to experiment and play.
6. Now you are ready to accompany a song. You start the singing and rub your hands together to indicate the rhythm. Any song or nursery rhyme with a simple rhythm will do.

Pen and Pencil Percussion

What you need

* pencils and pens - all different sizes and lengths, some with rubbers on the ends, some taped together in 3's or 4's.

Links with ELGs

CLL - Distinguish one sound from another.

CD - Respond & show an interest in what they hear. Explore and learn how sounds can be changed.

This activity is best done sitting in a group round a table.

2. Put all the pens and pencils in the middle of the table and invite the children to experiment freely with them to produce as many different sounds as they can.

3. Now take turns to perform the sounds you have invented. Recap on each sound - 'Stan has tapped his pen on the table,' or Nadia has rolled her pencil along the table top.' Make sure everyone has a chance to show their sounds.

4. Now start a rhythm yourself with one of the pencils. Encourage the children to join in and stop at a pre-arranged signal.

5. Offer one or two children a chance to start a rhythm for everyone else to copy.

6. You can use pencil percussion to accompany songs or CD music.

Try 'Carousel Nursery Rhymes' or 'Small Voices, Big Noises' - both CDs available from Featherstone Education

Bouncing Ball (suitable for older children)

This activity needs a large space, preferably inside.

1. This session can become quite energetic. Begin with a warm up eg a tall body shape that changes to a small ball shape. Give each child a ball and show them how to roll it around their waists, up and down their legs, etc. This gives the body a gentle stretch.
2. Ask the children to find a space and practice bouncing their ball in front of them. They can either sit or stand.
3. After a short time of exploration, ask the children to watch some demonstrations from others. Comment on how each child is maintain control of their ball.
4. Give them some more time to practice. Those who have mastered the first task could try moving around the space with the ball. They could be asked to stop and hold a 'bouncing' conversation with anyone they meet.
5. Bring the children into a circle in the middle of the space. Demonstrate by standing up with feet slightly apart a steady rhythm with a ball bounced down in front of you. Encourage the children to join in, one at a time, and keep a steady rhythm. Use a popular song to assist in this. The children could be tasked to turn around on the spot as they bounce.
6. End the session with a quiet 'cooling off' activity.

Links with ELGs

CD - Respond & show an interest in what they hear. Explore how sounds can be changed.

KUW - Show curiosity & interest by facial expression, movement, sound.

What you need

* a variety of balls, different sizes and 'bounce' - footballs, small rubber, Airflow, ping pong, 'koosh', fabric

31

Bucket Beat

Make a circle and place two buckets in the middle.

2. This is a call-and-response activity. You need to start it off!
3. Choose a child as a partner and go into the middle of the circle.
4. Play the bucket with your hand (at this early stage, three taps is enough).
5. With younger children, you could make up a short sentence which echoes your beat - eg

   Have you got a _dog_, a _great_ _big_ _dog_?

   or _I_ go _school_ _now_
5. Ask your partner to play back your rhythm on their bucket.
6. Play your rhythm again until the it is clearly established and steady.
7. Ask your partner to stay in the middle and choose another child to come and play the sound with them. Go around the circle in this way until everyone has had a go.

If you have two adults, you could divide the group and make two circles.

It is a lovely activity to play outside if you have the space and the weather!

Links with ELGs

CLL - Distinguish one sound from another

CD - Respond to sound with body movement. Explore how sounds can be changed.

What you need

*   2 small plastic buckets with handles (decorator's buckets are ideal. You can get them from a DIY store)

About Part 4

Part Four explores using the objects and materials in Part Three with a range of different objects as beaters. You will still need the following:
  * tabletops, trays, buckets, sandpaper
  * some simple hand percussion instruments, such as drums, tambours, claves and woodblocks

You will also need to collect the following things to use as beaters:

  * spoons (metal, plastic, wooden).
  * drinking straws and Art straws, sticks and twigs.
  * feathers (craft feathers don't need health checking!).
  * some carpet squares for individual children and to make quiet places for instruments.

Some of these things will be available in your setting, others may be available if you ask parents and carers, others will need to be 'researched' in charity shops and sales.

Part 4

Using Beaters

- using a variety of beaters to explore sound and rhythm.

Brilliant Beaters

What you need

* A collection of spoons
* Straws, feathers, twigs, sticks
* Untuned percussion instruments
* Carpet squares, pointing wand

Sit in a circle - it helps if each person has a carpet sample!

1. Put the instruments and beaters in the middle of the circle.
2. Let each child choose a percussion instrument and a beater, which they put on the carpet in front of them.

Younger children will need practice at this, and do better in groups of six or less.

3. Give the children some time to experiment with the instrument and beater they have chosen, stopping on your signal.
4. Now sing this song:

    Can you play with the spoons, the spoons, the spoons.
    Can you play with the spoons, the spoons, NOW?

    All the children with spoons play their instruments.
5. Now continue with *Can you play the feathers; the twigs; the straws etc* till everyone has had a go.
6. Talk about the different sounds, and jot down some of the words the children use to describe the sounds. This could be a good basis for a music display with some of your 'found' beaters and sound makers.

Another idea

Why not record some of your music sessions and add the recording to your display? You could also take some photos of the children and their instruments.

Let's Have a Parade (Part 1)

Put all these activities together and have a parade round your room, the garden, the school or even your neighbourhood. Celebrate a festival or just do it for fun!

1. Get together with the children and make a plan.
2. Decide what sort of parade you will have and what sort of music you will play. You could make a Chinese Dragon, celebrate Carnival, Divali or Harvest, have a band or any other idea the children may have.
3. Make a list of all the things you need to do for the parade. You may need costumes, head-dresses or masks. You may need to make or find some more sound makers.
4. Younger children will probably want to have the parade immediately. Older children may like to make some posters or notices to publicise the parade to any potential audience.
5. You will need to practice walking in a marching line (a drum or tambour is useful for practising this), and you will need to practice the music!
6. Don't forget to take some photos of the parade for a display or album.

Planning and doing a parade touches on almost every area of learning

More about parades on pages 58 and 59.

About Part 5

Preparing for the next section may involve a little expense or ingenuity! You need to collect the following objects:

* corks, shells, pebbles, gravel
* combs, brushes and brooms of all sorts and sizes (hair, dog, shoe, paint, washing up, nail, scrubbing etc).
* hand and foot pumps (bicycle balloon, garden).
* plungers (these come in many sizes).
* newspapers, plastic bottles.
* packs of cards.
* clean old clothes, sheets, blankets, pieces of fabric.
* balloons.

The children and their families may be able to donate some of the things you need. Others will need to be bought from the cheapest available source!

Part 5

Exploring sound and rhythm

- using everyday objects and materials to make music

I Got Rhythm!

Links with ELGs

CLL - Distinguish one sound from another.

CD - Respond to sound with body movement, show an interest in what they hear. Explore and learn how sounds can be changed.

What you need

* Brushes and combs of different types and sizes
* Corks
* Sticks, twigs, pencils etc

This is an excellent activity for experimentation and discovery. By varying the shape and size of the tray and the depth of material in it, quite different sounds can be produced.

1. Put gravel, sand or pebbles in some different trays or bowls (plant saucers, washing up bowls, plastic boxes). Some bowls of each works well to extend the range of sounds and rhythms. Try individual bowls as well as bigger ones to share.

2. Offer a collection of brushes, combs, corks etc for making rhythms.

3. Let the children explore the materials and instruments freely.

4. Now ask for demonstrations of different sounds and rhythms. Encourage rhythms by demonstrating one of your own or one of theirs for others to copy.

5. Talk about the movements of the instruments and the different sounds they make. Exchange containers or instruments to get a new sound.

6. If the children are ready, try incorporating several sounds and rhythms into a story or a composition. You could also have an orchestra to accompany singing or recorded music. Choose pieces with a strong beat.

Pump up the Volume!

This activity is great fun, but be aware that some children are scared of balloons.

1. Fill some plastic bottles and a washing up bowl with water.
2. Sit in a circle with the children - pumps and other things in the centre.
3. Demonstrate how each of the pumps works (first with the end out of the water, then with the end or connector under the water or in the neck of an empty balloon. This is sure to induce great merriment!
4. Ask for some volunteers to work some of the pumps.
5. Stand up with the rest of the children, and explain that you are going to be a machine. Start a rhythmical movement(eg swinging your arms and counting 1, 2; bending and straightening your knees to 1, 2; lifting and lowering one leg; pushing your fists out, then in).
6. The pumpers must pump in time with your rhythm. Keep it slow and steady.

    Foot pumpers may need help with balance!

7. Using an agreed signal, slow the 'machine' down to a stop.

Links with ELGs

CLL- Distinguish one sound from another.

CD - Respond to sound with body move ment, show an interest in what they hear. Explore and learn how sounds can be changed.

What you need

* A selection of pumps (foot, bike, garden) with and without adaptors.
* Plastic bottles and bowls
* Balloons (not inflated)

Take the Plunge

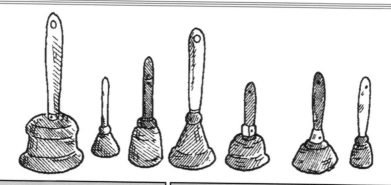

What you need

* As many plungers as you can collect!
* A clean, smooth floor.

Links with ELGs

CLL - Distinguish one sound from another.
CD - Respond to sound with body movement.
Explore & learn how sounds can be changed.

Plungers come in all shapes, colours and sizes, some are small enough for even the smallest hands to use. Make sure they are new, or they have been sterilised in a dishwasher.

1. Resist the temptation to add water to this activity, as you will end up with a scene from a terrible plumbing disaster! You need a smooth clean floor for best results.
2. Sit in a circle and put the plungers in the middle.
3. Get the children to put their hands over their mouths and suck in air, so they know how plungers work.
4. Now pass the plungers around so everyone can see the different sorts and sizes.
5. Ask the children if they know what plungers are for and how they work. If someone knows, get them to demonstrate. If not, you need to do it yourself, using the floor as a surface.
6. The children will love the sucking sound - let them try!
7. When the children have all had a go and a good laugh, listen to the different sounds made by different plungers. Encourage words like loud/soft, higher/lower.

Wetting the rim of the plunger will increase the volume of the sound!

Brushes and Brooms

Sit or stand in a circle with all the brooms and brushes in the middle.

2. Demonstrate the sound each broom can make (or ask a volunteer to help)

3. Now invite each child to choose a brush or broom and experiment to see how many sounds they can make with it.

4. Next you can make a sound with your brush and see if they can copy you. If they can, try a short sequence of sounds or get them to make a sound for you to copy.

Another idea

Try accompanying 'Here we go Round the Mulberry Bush' with your broom sounds.

> *This is the way we scrub the floor,*
> *Scrub the floor,*
> *Scrub the floor.*
> *This is the way we scrub the floor,*
> *On a cold and frosty morning.*

OR you could give your brushers some 'Rhythmic moving' instructions such as 'skating feet', 'stamping feet', 'sliding feet', 'crunching feet'.

Links with ELGs

CLL - Distinguish one sound from another.
CD - Respond to sound with body movement, show an interest in what they hear. Explore & learn how sounds can be changed.

What you need

* A number of stiff brushes & brooms
* A smooth floor, inside or out

Water, Water Everywhere!

1. Get the children to help you fill the bottles to different levels with blue coloured water (a funnel helps!). Tiny amounts are just as effective as larger amounts.
2. Screw the caps on securely, taping any that are risky (silver or black duct tape is waterproof and provides a good seal).
3. let the children experiment with different ways of making sounds with the bottles - shaking, swishing, tapping with fingers, knocking on the floor. Give demonstrations if they need help.
4. Get some of the children to perform their sounds.
5. Sing and accompany some water songs such as 'A Sailor Went to Sea,' or 'Bobby Shaftoe'.

Another idea

Make a storm in a bottle. Hold the bottles on their sides, and keep still to make a calm sea. Gradually tilt the bottle to make waves. Describe the storm starting as the children make more and more violent movements of their own 'sea in a bottle'.

Bring the sea back to calm by reversing the order of your commentary till calm is restored.

Links with ELGs	What you need
CLL - Distinguish one sound from another. CD - Respond to sound with body movement, show an interest in what they hear. Explore and learn how sounds can be changed.	* Plastic bottles filled to different levels with water; funnel * Blue food colouring

44

Newspaper Noises

Newspaper is an under-used sound maker!

Newspaper has a wonderful sound making quality that is very versatile - it can be:

* rolled into lengths and used as a beater
* scrunched up into a ball and thrown between people
* torn, in long slow strips or in short loud ones.

Hand out some newspaper to each child (both broadsheet and tabloid, as each will give a different sustain). Use your magic wand/pointer/conductor's baton, to orchestrate the children's music by pointing at them.

1. Work with the children to experiment with different ways of making sounds with the newspaper. You can scrunch and shake the paper, you could tear it in long strips or short pieces, or you could roll it up and tape it to make beaters and sticks.

Another idea

The children could work in pairs - one holding a sheet of paper while the other one taps, shakes, pats, scrunches it. They could also use brushes, small sticks, pencils, leaves etc to alter the sounds.

Fix sheets over empty cans, tins, tubes for home-made drums.

Play the Game

Links with ELGs
CLL - Distinguish one sound from another.
CD - Respond to sound with body movement, show an interest in what they hear. Explore and learn how sounds can be changed.

What you need
* Playing cards
* Things to tap on them

Packs of cards are cheap, easily obtained and fun to use for sound making.

Here are some quick ideas:

1. Take a bunch of cards and flap, flick or run a thumb across the edges.
2. Share out the cards and take turns to put them down, keeping a steady rhythm (easier for older and more dextrous children, but a really good fine motor activity!)
3. Hold a card in one hand and tap, flick or pat it with the other hand or a finger. Try different rhythms, or use a stick or paintbrush to get a different sound.
4. Try 'card ski-ing' across a table, carpet, floor, grass or patio by flicking with one finger to make a slithering sound.
5. Drop a bunch of cards on different surfaces to make rain, waterfalls, footsteps or other sounds. Try the floor, carpet, the surface of a drum, a piece of newspaper, foil.
6. Hold a card in each hand and tap or flick them together to accompany songs and rhymes.

Another idea

If the children can work in pairs, have a card in each hand and use them to make a rhythm with a partner by tapping, flicking, patting etc.

Musical Outfits

Put all the clothes in a basket or box in the middle of the carpet. Make sure all the clothes are clean!

1. Take turns to take something out of the basket and experiment with how it can make sounds. You could:

    bang, flick, tap, use buttons and zips to beat on the floor
    flick legs, socks, scarves in the air
    bang two shoes together
    flip the flippers, flop the flops
    zip the zippers up and down, pop the poppers
    click the belt buckles, tap buttons together

2. When you have explored all the sounds, children can take their favourite item and join in a song such as:

    We can play on the trouser belt, and this is the way we do it,
    Tap, tap, tap on the trouser belt and this is the music to it.
    We can play on the swimming flippers and this is the way we do it,
    Slap, slap, slap on the swimming flippers, this is the music to it.

Another idea

Use your costume orchestra to accompany records, tapes, CDs of nursery rhymes, songs or other music with a strong beat.

Links with ELGs

CLL - Distinguish one sound from another.
CD - Respond to sound with body movement, show an interest in what they hear. Explore and learn how sounds can be changed.

What you need

* As many different items of clothing as you can find - trousers, socks, shoes, things with zips and poppers, belts, buckles, flip flops, flippers, rubber gloves, wellies etc.

Get a Feel For Fabrics

These items are usually readily available in settings. For a different range, try a Fabricadabra pack from Featherstone Education.

1. Make sure you have plenty of space.
2. Put the fabrics in the middle of the circle or on a table.
2. Take turns to experiment with the sounds and movements they can make - try wafting, snapping, shaking, rubbing, fats and slow movements.
3. Choose some songs with different moods and rhythms to accompany with the fabrics. Try songs about the sea, nursery rhymes with pace and rhythm, animal rhymes.
4. Put some music on a CD or tape player and make movements with the fabrics to the rhythms and beat.
5. Try taking the fabrics outside and making your fabric music into a dance or procession.

Another idea

Try using your fabrics to accompany chants, songs and stories. Try using your magic wand (a stick) and saying "Magic wand, Magic wand, make a stormy sound. Magic wand, Magic, wand, make a soothing sound." Or use the sounds to accompany stories such as The Rainbow Fish, A Balloon for Grandad, Where the Wild Things Are, The Little Boat.

Links with ELGs

CLL - Distinguish one sound from another.
CD - Respond to sound with body movement, show an interest in what they hear. Explore and learn how sounds can be changed.

What you need

* Sheets, blankets, pieces of fabric, scarves, ribbons

Part 6

Creating Sound Environments

- using music, sound and rhythm to create stories and sound environments in your setting
- making instruments to use in your stories

In the Playground

This activity uses equipment for physical development to make a musical setting. You can do this activity indoors or in the garden. You need PE equipment such as balls of various sizes & sorts, skipping ropes, hoops, bean bags etc.

1. Start by playing with the equipment and exploring the sorts of sounds each thing can make. Encourage the children to experiment by bouncing, dropping, tapping, slapping, rubbing. Older children could practice skipping rhythmically (this is hard!), younger ones could turn a rope between two, or with an adult.
2. Now the children should choose one piece of equipment and get into pairs or groups with the same equipment(like an orchestra or band).
3. Get them to practice together, then each group to play in turn. This may be enough for some groups! Stop if they get frustrated or bored.

Taking it further

The Sound of Outdoors

Ask for ideas about the kind of sounds children hear when playing outside. Make sure that each group has enough space to work in and allow some time for them to practice their sound. While you are aiming for an overall effect, it may be enough for each group to 'play', their piece alone. The main purpose is to lead very young children towards the idea of playing as part of a whole - persevere!

Use your magic wand to orchestrate, beginning with one group to set up a steady rhythm. Add the another group, and then (if all goes well) introduce a hand clapping group with individuals or pairs clapping together.

Finally you could add a chant such as Oranges and lemons or Ring-a Ring of Roses.

The Party Sound

This idea can be repeated using the theme of a party. Parties give lots of opportunities for songs and games

Sounds of the Sea

A seaside theme can draw on activities from elsewhere in this book, combining several to make a sound tapestry. Try Sandpaper Sounds, Bucket Beat, Combs in Sand (customised by including trays of shells), Bottles of Water and Sheets and Blankets.

Forest Fun

A Rainforest soundscape could incorporate work already covered in Jungle Sounds, Rainstorm, Bottles of Water and Newspaper.

Rainsticks (bought or made following the instructions in this book) also give great depth to this sound environment.

Trains and boats and planes (and cars)

You could play the same game with vehicle sounds, including bike bells, horns, hooters, sirens and wheels.

Weather Reports

Use all the sounds you have found to make rain, storms, thunder, lightning, wind, snow, hail and sun. Use the sounds to accompany weather songs and rhymes.

Let's go on a Bear Hunt!

Using a story to inspire a soundscape

'We're Going on a Bear Hunt ^ by Michael Rosen and Helen Oxenbury
A much-acclaimed classic that many children will already be familiar with. This activity is designed to tease out the musical and rhythmical qualities of the text.

You need a collection of the sound makers you have handy - brushes, water in bottles, suckers and plungers, fabric pieces etc. Put all these in a box or basket in the middle of the circle.

1. Read the story with the children (even if they have heard it before, they will love the retelling.

2. Focus specifically on the movements and expressive language used to describe each obstacle that the family faces as they go off on their hunt.

   Use an expressive tone and emphasise the grass 'swishy, swashy'; the river 'splash, splosh'; the mud 'squelch, squerch'; the snowstorm 'hooo, wooo'; the forest 'stumble, trip'; the cave 'tiptoe, tiptoe'.

   Each has a lovely sense of movement and rhythm and a retelling of the story with rehearsed sound effects will add a new dimension to it.

   The first step in making the soundscape is to decide on individuals, pairs or groups to make each of the sounds. Give them the chance to say the words over and over and add a movement to them. This allows them to get to grips with the task ahead and also helps to suggest how they might play their instruments or sound makers.

3. Now each sound needs an instrument or sound maker. let the children experiment and decide which ones they would like to use. More reticent children may need a suggestion from others or from an adult, but give them a chance to do it themselves first. Try not to show your own preferences - accept theirs, even though they may seem strange!

You could also help them to invent more sounds such as:
* sandpaper rubbed gently together or newspapers being opened and closed in time with the words could suggest 'Swishy, swashy'
* bottles of water, timed to be played on each word could be used for 'Splash, splosh'
* Squelch, squerch, allows the children the opportunity of making a raspberry noise by blowing hard on the back of their hands or they could use plungers
* 'Hooo, wooo' gives the challenge of making stormy noises without masking the words - sheets and blankets can be used here, while blowing and whistling sounds can be made by the remainder of the group
* 'Stumble, trip' can be represented by customising part of the Clever Clapping/Super Stamping routine, accentuating the syllables of each word with two thumps of the chest and one clap of the hands. You could add the Bucket Beat idea for extra volume!
* finally, 'Tiptoe, tiptoe' can be realised by using a version of Rainstorm - the two fingers clapped into the palm of the hand for a quiet sound. A lot of fun can be had by raising the tempo for each of these as the family rush back home pursued by the bear!

Let's celebrate again!

Processions and parades are a really good way of celebrating any event in your setting - try some of these!

While there are many opportunities for presentation during the school year, it may be worth considering introducing the idea or a parade or procession at regular intervals in your class. It will enliven and celebrate the uniqueness of the children and combine to assist their learning and understanding. You could:

Celebrate birthdays

Try a musical birthday procession. The child whose birthday it is decides:

1. The kind of instruments they want in their procession (buckets, tambours, bottles of water etc);
2. Where they want to lead the procession (just around the room, into the parallel class, through the school - this may need a warning to your colleagues beforehand! - or into the playground);
3. Whether there will be flags and banners etc.
   You set the rhythm for everyone to follow. The chant of 'Have you got a dog, a great big dog?' is useful here.
   Also introduce the idea of a 360 degree turn regularly throughout the procession. This is a staple of all good carnival parades from New Orleans to Rio.

Celebrate the end of a topic or centre of interest

Have a colour parade, a minibeasts parade, a hot and cold parade where children play rhythms, sing songs and carry items associated with the topic.

Celebrate special days

All sorts of celebrations, festivals and special days can be excuses for parades - Chinese new Year, Divali, Christmas, Spring, Carnival, Harvest etc. Each one will have its own special colours, rhythms, songs and sounds.

Celebrate successes and achievements

How about a good work parade or a being kind parade?

Celebrate occasions in your setting or school

Have a parade to celebrate a new building, a new classroom, new furniture and equipment, new staff and children. Celebrate being in a new group, or the last day in your old one. Celebrate the blossom on the trees, the bulbs coming up, the snow coming down, the tadpoles turning into frogs, some body's new baby or new pet - in fact anything worth celebrating is worth a parade!!

and finally

We now know that movement helps learning. Use music, rhythm, songs, parades and celebrations to help children learn. Brain breaks, clapping, stamping, tapping and playing simple instruments all help develop the brain as well as being good for muscle control.

......and a couple of instruments to make

Making rain sticks

The rain stick is a South American or African instrument that sounds just like pouring rain. It is very easy to make and is an extremely useful tool to have in your setting.

Authentic rain sticks consist of a hollow wooden tube with wooden cross-spokes inside. The tube is then filled with beans, seeds, beads or small stones. When tilted the seeds run down the length of the tube, hitting the cross-spokes as they fall. This creates a remarkably realistic and at the same time musical rain sound.

Here is a very inexpensive way to make your own rain stick:
What you need for each child:
  * 2 or 3 kitchen towel tubes (you could use aluminium foil or other long tubes if you want a longer length)
  * a large quantity of toothpicks for each stick
  * masking tape
  * wrapping or other coloured paper/plastic to cover your sticks
  * multicoloured rubber bands
  * lolly sticks
  * drawing pin
  * small objects such as lentils/beans/seeds, etc.

What you do:

1. Tape the tubes together to make one longer tube if you need to.
2. Reinforce the joins well with the masking tape.
3. Decorate the tubes brightly as desired.
4. Cover one end of the tube with the paper or plastic wrap held in place by a rubber band covered with masking tape.
5. Use the drawing pin to make holes down the length of the tube about 3 to 4 cm apart in a spiral pattern.
6. Now blunt the sharp ends of a toothpick by pressing on to the table. Younger children will need help with this or you may want to blunt all the toothpicks before you start.
7. Push the end of one of the toothpicks into one of the holes in the tube as far as it will go.
8. Keep doing this until all the holes are filled. The more toothpicks you use the more convincing the rain sound.
9. Pour in lentils etc. Cover the end securely with paper or plastic wrap and seal as before.

Try some experiments with other sizes of seeds, fewer toothpicks, longer or shorter lengths of tube.

Now you have a Rain stick band!

Squawking parrots!

Try making some of these noisy sound makers to add to your music sessions.

Parrots, like many other creatures in rainforests, communicate with each other by sound. The following activity allows children to replicate this squawking and create a flock of parrots for in your room.

What you need for each child:
* some colour pictures of parrots for reference and ideas
* plastic cups (brightly coloured if possible)
* string
* pieces of sponge
* thin card or paper in bright colours
* craft feathers (optional),
* marker pens and one permanent pen
* glue, drawing pins, pencil, scissors

What you do:
1. Using a drawing pin, poke a small hole in the centre bottom of the cup.
2. Widen the hole with the scissors or the point of a pencil. (Be careful not to split the cup).
3. Cut a length of string and push it through the hole and then knot it.
4. Glue the knot into place and then leave to dry.

5. Meanwhile, decorate the cup with card or coloured paper cut to look like feathers - or you could use the craft feathers.
6. Cut out a beak and stick it on the head.
7. Draw in the eyes with a marker pen, or cut some out and stick them on.
8. Now wet the piece of sponge and tie it to the string on the cup and let it dangle. This gives tautness to the string and keeps it moist, producing a louder sound.
9. Take the string between your index finger and thumb and slide them down length of string. This should produce a squawking sound that is amplified by the size and shape of the cup.

You could also experiment with different sized cups and thicknesses of string.

Happy Squawking!!

don't forget....

You can make instruments from all sorts of simple 'junk' or recycled objects.

Hear are some ideas of things to collect - if you offer these to the children they will experiment and come up with a huge range of different combinations of sounds and materials.

Recycled objects:
* yogurt pots and plastic cups
* plastic washing up liquid and pop bottles
* string
* foam, sticks, cardboard tubes
* old saucepans, kettles, teapots
* wooden and metal spoons, forks, ladles etc.
* the outer tubes of old felt pens with the felt removed
* boxes, tins, cans
* lids, tops
* stones, gravel, sand, leaves, twigs, seeds
* wood offcuts
* foil dishes
* newspaper
* tissue paper and paper bags

Cheap things (try Pound Shops and DIY centres):
* thin chain
* rope
* beans, buttons, pasta shapes, lentils etc
* buckets, bowls, plant pots, plastic and metal tubing
* sandpaper blocks
* dowel, plant sticks, short canes

and use your junk orchestra every day!

Once you and the children have got used to making your own sound makers, use every opportunity to accompany songs, rhymes, stories and other activities with simple sounds and music.

We now know that children who can
* use both hands together,
* imagine and create,
* maintain a beat,
* move in rhythm,
* work together,

learn more, learn faster
and love learning!